T0196947

Materialism
in the
Baptist Church
due to
Spiritual
Warfare

KARENE TAYLOR-THORNE

A CAPSTONE PROJECT

Submitted to
New York Theological Seminary
in partial fulfillment of the requirements
for the degree of

MASTERS OF ARTS IN PASTORAL
CARE AND COUNSELING

WESTBOW
PRESS®
A DIVISION OF THOMAS NELSON
& ZONDERVAN

WestBow Press books may be ordered through booksellers or by contacting:

WestBow Press
A Division of Thomas Nelson & Zondervan
1663 Liberty Drive
Bloomington, IN 47403
www.westbowpress.com
1 (866) 928-1240

ISBN: 978-1-5127-5102-4 (sc)
ISBN: 978-1-5127-5103-1 (e)

Print information available on the last page.

WestBow Press rev. date: 8/9/2016

Abstract

IS MATERIALISM IN THE BAPTIST CHURCH THE RESULT OF SPIRITUAL WARFARE

By

KARENE TAYLOR-THORNE

The abstract of my project seek to know if materialism in the Baptist Church is the result of Spiritual Warfare. Materialism is defined by Webster dictionary as putting too much emphasis on material goods such as clothing, cars, electronic devices and anything that brings much comfort, while not paying attention to spiritual or intellectual values. Is it the result of Spiritual Warfare or human greed? Spiritual Warfare is the leading of the evil force influencing people to do evil. There exist in this world two forces, good and bad. They are in opposition to each other. Human existence will endure attacks of evil in this world that is influenced by the bad force. After conversion they are to mature and reject their former lifestyle by showing love, truth, forgiveness, sexual purity and not being greedy. We do not fight against flesh and blood, but evil forces in high places. The problem is not with man or woman but with the one who controls the evil forces. Church will be led by the good or bad force. God or Satan.

Contents

Introduction

My capstone project is on the topic of Materialism in the Baptist Church due to Spiritual Warfare. Are we consumed with our own agenda and leaving behind what the church was instituted for? Has time brought about new purposes of the church? Are we to worship human beings and not the creator of the Universe?

- Statement of the problem: Is Materialism in the Baptist Church the result of Spiritual Warfare?
- It is significant for the survival of the Church and for members to examine whether they are true to self and have renewed their mind.

  My interest was sparked by observing excess in the church. Fashion, money, intelligence, eloquence and influence seemed to be the measuring rod for success and promotion. The spiritual component was now hiding behind natural and humanistic values.

  The topic is important for me and the community and the field of pastoral care and counseling to enlighten us and encourage us to let go of the greed and be true to self and take responsibility for our bad decisions. If the counselor is not true to self, clients will be lead in the wrong way.

My project will encourage the reader to examine him or herself and know that after conversion they should live a different lifestyle. They too will learn that life will bring about good and bad because of the two forces, good and evil.

Evil forces are influencing Church people to greed and ungodly character. They live the same life that they did before coming to the church. The church is concerned with money and popularity and is leaning towards a natural environment rather than a spiritual environment.

- The method of my project included interviews with young and old members of the church.

Materialism suggest that we can't seem to overcome the desire to shop and accumulate things. Is the buying frenzy what makes us feel good, hence a form of therapy or is it just habituated greed? We do have to take responsibility for our actions, but I do believe that we are engaged in spiritual warfare also. According to Ephesians 6:12, it is not the human being (flesh and blood) that we struggle against, but against cosmic powers of darkness. Paul wrote a letter encouraging the Ephesian to mature and to let go of their former lifestyles. They needed to have different values such as love, truth, forgiveness, sexual purity and not be greedy for material things.

Paul is trying to make the people understand the difference between doctrine and what it looks like in real life. He also said that because people are not perfect they would be attacked by that bad or evil force at some time in life. The church is to insure God's rule over creation. Humanistic plans and world views should not be permitted in the church. If God is not leading the church it is led by Satan.[1]

Let us reflect on the biblical scripture found in John 2:13-16, which tells us about Jesus celebrating the Passover season in Jerusalem. Jesus found people selling oxen, sheep, doves and they were concerned only with material gain. He became very angry and drove them out of the temple. According to Obery Hendricks, the temple had become an economic institution where the priestly aristocracy represented Roman interests—including financial interests. Jesus did not approve of the people making the temple a place of commercialization rather than of worship.[2] Many Baptist Churches use the place of worship for commercial use to raise money by selling cakes, chicken dinners or sponsoring trips.

The problem of materialism in the church due to evil or bad forces is tough for the field of pastoral care and

---

[1] E.M.Bounds,*Guide To Spiritual Warfare* (New Kensington, PA: Whitaker House,1984),51.

[2] Obery Hendricks, *The Politics of Jesus* (NewYork, NY: Three Leaves Press, 2006), 114.

counseling and to me, because one can't easily measure evil forces. Poling has an interesting concept on evil. Evil arises out of life and it is not outside of the bodies or spirits. There are power struggles between people because the desire is to be more powerful than the next person, which leads to treating them as objects. We tend to categorize people and consider people who are different than we are to be less important, and not loved by the supreme power. Evil is the result of sin that turns us away from self, God and others. He too states that it is hard to discern good from evil because it often parades as good. Counselors can easily be caught in this web and misjudge people.[3]

As I assess how evil forces in the church are leading to materialism, I need to be critical and aware of my own shortcomings so that I can judge fairly as a pastoral counselor engaged with clients in social and cultural situations. A pastor must be grounded in spiritual knowledge and truth in order to handle power dynamics when relating to a client.

I believe that the higher power that I look to led me to this topic. One morning after completing a two-day fast I awakened with the name E.M. Bounds in my mouth. I was familiar with him because I have a book written by him on *Spiritual Warfare*. I hurriedly went to my bookcase and the book was in my hands in a few seconds. The book described in detail the personality of the invisible enemy, Satan, and

[3] Carrie Doehring, *The,(Practice of PastoralCare: a post modern approach,(Kentucky:* Louisville, Westminister John Knox Press, 2006), 127-128.

how he is subverting the Church through deception.[4] I did not understand what this subject matter had to do with me and my life at the time. I did feel that I was to bring new light to this subject.

All people will battle between flesh and spirit. The evil force draws us into wrong behaviors such as envy and selfishness. It does not mean that we lose Salvation, but will live a life in spiritual battle. Counselors will try to impress the very people they are to serve with their charm, ability, wealth and leadership, thereby shutting down the client. There would be no sacrifice of self in order to serve others and minister to their needs. Counselors must be good listeners and be able to put themselves in the shoes of those they seek to help, while at the same time keeping good boundaries by holding their own feelings and thoughts. A carnal minded counselor could end up fusing with a client and not see things clearly. The client is already vulnerable so it is the responsibility of the counselor to set healthy limits. At the extreme the Pastor will become a false teacher and instead of helping clients will lead them away from God or whatever higher power they look to.

Evil forces are having great influence on the major socialization agents in our society, such as family, school, church, law, work, peer groups and education. As the postmodern society becomes more isolated, television advertisements are received consciously and unconsciously. Education is desired and can bring new and better ways

---

[4] Bounds, *Guide to Spiritual Warfare* (New Kensington, PA; Whitaker House, 1984), 51.

of doing things. The postmodern approach is a very good example because it includes race, gender, context and culture.[5] This is all because of materialism. Materialism is the pursuit of happiness through the consumption of goods and money. Acquiring things is important to materialist, it brings happiness and well-being and lastly it is a status symbol.

[5] Carrie Doehring, *The, (Practice of Pastoral Care: a post modern approach,(Kentucky:* Louisville, Westminister John Knox Press, 2006), 167.

Review of Literature

According to the article found in *Truth Magazine,* Webster defines materialism as having too much emphasis on material interests. The author looks at Timothy 5:8, which states that whoever does not provide for family members is worse than an unbeliever and has denied the faith. We are expected to work with our hands to meets our earthly needs. Lazy people who don't want to work should not eat and the church should not feed them. The excessive need to possess things is idolatry. Focusing on earthly treasures he states, means that we are bowing before the god of riches. His second definition of materialism is to enjoy oneself to the extreme and this is materialism as well as selfishness.[6]

A very popular rock song of the seventies starts with the words, "There's a Lady who's sure all that glitters is gold

---

[6] CecilWillis, "Problems in the Church(III): Materialism". *Truth Magazine,* November, 1962,http:/Trurhmagazine.com/archieves/volume7/TM007013.htm. (assessed November4, 2014).

and she's buying a stairway to heaven."[7] The message was against materialism that had become the backbone of rock music in the sixties and seventies. The group Led Zeppelin, sought to encourage people to seek the sacred or that which has eternal value.[8] We are to seek our creator rather than things that last a short time.

The book by Bruce Shelley, *The Gospel and The American Dreamer,* depicts a man who said that he would be a millionaire by age 35. He was successful as he flew from Phoenix to Dallas weekly on business. He owned the best car and lived in the best neighborhood. Suddenly his job was gone and his pride and image was destroyed. After his family went to bed he placed his insurance policy where it was easy to find. He went into his garage and got into his car and turned on the ignition and succumbed to the poisonous gases.[9] He did not reach his full potential because he was consumed with things that he considered to be status symbols. His family would spend the rest of their lives wishing that he was with them rather than having material things.

We have a story of a man who had a good job working for a large firm. He put his money into a 401 (K) that could

---

[7] DonClosson, "*TheStairway to Heaven:Materialism and the Church,* http://www.leaderu.com/orgs/probe/docs/stairway.html.(assessed November4, 2014).

[8] ibid.

[9] Bruce Shelley, *The Gospel and The American Dreamer: The Millionaire and The Dreamer,* http://www.leaderu.com/orgs/probe/docs/stairway.html (assessed November4, 2014).

have been used to fund his retirement years. He left his high paying job to teach at a Christian college. His passion was to buy an old house for Students who wanted to know God better and wanted to share with people who shared the same idea. This house cost him his savings but he was living his dream. He renovated the house so that graduate and undergraduate students could live there. He held Bible study and reading groups at this house. He was very happy about working for God .[10] This man is optimistic even though his dream lacks good business plans. He was not consumed with material things for himself, but wanted to help others find peace and love in the sacred.

The International Journal of Business and Social Science, states that as a person ages he or she will focus less on material possessions. As children become adults they tend to share their things. A study was done to measure three elements of materialism such as possessiveness, envy and generosity. Possessiveness and generosity are related to the age of those studied. Envy was not as prevalent as one aged because they had achieved material goals. Materialism was the result of feelings of insecurity and from social influences such as advertisements. Self-esteem was a factor in determining why children sought after material things. A low self-esteem drove one to acquire things to feel better about him or herself.[11]

---

[10] Ibid,2.

[11] *International Journal of Business and Socia lScience: "Ageand Materialism": Vol.2* No.23 (2011) 241.

We live in a postmodern society whereby individuals are alienated and easily influenced by social agents like consumer socialization. Ward (1974a) defines consumer socialization as the process by which young people learn and form attitudes as consumers. Television and family interaction play a major role in developing materialistic values in young adults. Belk (1984) proposes that materialism in extreme provided much satisfaction and dissatisfaction. A child's purchasing power is related to how the family communicated. The first dimension-socio-orientation is vertical communication and indicates hierarchical interaction (McLeod & Chaffee). The child's consumption is controlled and monitored. The second dimension is concept-orientation and it considers the child's input and seek to provide an environment to stimulate his/her own view. Parents who have high socio-orientation and high concept-orientation encourage their children to have independent ideas. Low-socio-orientation and low

Concept-orientation induce low levels of communication. At this point children are greatly influenced by external socialization agents such as the media.[12]

Dr. Gene Getz, a Cuban pastor stated in his book *A Biblical Theology of Material Possessions* that believers can be in bondage to things. People in Cuba have few things and lots of time. He states that if our focus is on things we spend our time buying, using, fixing, which does not allow us time

---

[12] *Internal Journal of Business and Social Science:Family Communication and Materialism*, Vol.2 No.23(Special Issue-December 2011), 240-241.

to be in relationships with people to spread the Gospel. We can't serve things and God. Financial power opens the door to economic injustice and oppression. He refers to Acts 8. He believes that some people will use the church for their own benefit. This was present in the beginning of the Church age and still exist today. He warns against self-indulgence and the desire for too much money. We are to seek contentment and not riches. When we are blessed with material good we should use it to further the Kingdom of God.[13]

---

[13] Gene Getz, *A Biblical Theology of Material Possessions: Material Possessions and the Church*, http://www.leaderu.com/orgs/probe/docs/stairway.html (assessed November 4, 2014).

Context of the project

The context of my research project focusing on materialism in the church due to spiritual warfare is challenging and with limits because the topic stirs fear and unbelief in many people. I will consider who is affected, and how decisions are made.

The church in which I will be conducting interviews is Bethany Baptist Church, in the community of Bedford-Stuyvesant in Brooklyn, New York. It is home to a diverse population that has been undergoing many changes. African-American professionals moved into the area in the year 1990 to 2000. They were working-class and lower middle-class. It was the area's first wave of gentrification. Between the years 2000 and 2010, the percentage of white residents increased from 2.4 percent to 15 percent, with a corresponding reduction among black residents of 15 percent, from 75 percent to 60, according to the census. Another wave of gentrification is ongoing. Europeans and Germans were said to be the original builders of the area are now returning. The living quarters are varied. They include two-family row-houses, brownstones of three floors.

Those brownstones are often divided up into apartments, with eight to twelve units in what were once two-family homes. In 2010 a couple bought a 19th century townhouse on Jefferson for $775k. The famous Boys and Girls High School averaged a score of 368 in reading, 362 in math, and 352 in writing in 2013. Citywide scores averaged 437 in reading, 463 in math, and 433 in writing. In 2013 the two precincts reported 19 murders versus 120 in 1990. There are many trains which makes a trip into New York City easy. The older generation dominate most Churches. Block parties and street festivals are frequent.[14]

WHO IS AFFECTED BY MATERIALISM

The church body or congregation is affected by materialism in the church. The backbone of the church are the elderly people who have been in the church for fifty years or more. Income ranges from low to moderate with a few members being wealthy. The older people are staying but attendance is down and they are very unhappy. Time has brought about many changes. The new Pastor has a new agenda. Inclusion of all people, rich, poor or marginalized are welcomed. The question we must ask is where does personal comfort end and the commitment to the cost of spreading the gospel begin? It is believed that fifty percent of money given to support the church came

---

[14] Diverse and Changing History",New York Times, July 13, 2014.

from baby boomers, born 1946-1964.[15] The millennial generation (born after 1984) are said to be materialistic. They desire the best of everything and are willing to pay the most. One home or one car is not enough. They grew up having everything because both parents worked. They expect to continue the lavish lifestyle. They are the biggest consumers of electronics.[16] If the millennials have so much material goods why don't they give more to keeping their church functioning? Their dress code is very casual.

As Christians we are not expected to conform to the ways of the world, but rather be transformed by the renewing of our minds, which is done by studying the Bible, prayer and reading. We then would seek to do the will of God.

The church has a diaconate board that makes the governing decisions along with the Pastor. It is a check and balance issue. The congregation is granted power that is unreal because they vote for who is most popular and accomplished. The desired outcome of the project is for the church to remain spiritual rather than become purely natural. The world is humanity that is separated from God and is concerned with earthly riches and pleasures. James 4:4 instructs us that friendship with the world is an enemy of God. We have to be aware of Satan's tricks because he

---

[15] Edward H, Hammett with James R. Pierce, *REACHING People under 40 while KEEPING People over 60* (St. Louis, MISSOURI: CHALICE PRESS, 2007), 38-39.

[16] Ibid,43.

will seek to bring about a counterfeit religion. Worship and ceremonies should be natural and spiritual.

Many Americans believe that God exist but live outside of his Will. They measure success on the basis of material gain. Human beings will war between the Spirit and flesh. Galatians 5:17 reminds us of Paul's writing, that the nature of man is sinful and wants that which is contrary to the Spirit and the Spirit wants that which is contrary to the sinful nature. One consumed by materialistic desires, lacks Spiritual depth. A person who does not receive the Holy Spirit is loss because it is necessary for a regenerate Spirit.

Theological Perspective

The Baptist Church accepts the Bible as their authority and depend on some traditions as accepted norms. We consider the Bible to be the approved word of God that becomes alive. It is by which we judge real life situations. We do have to consider proper exegesis of the scripture and understand that the books were written many centuries ago in different languages and cultures. Jesus used parables to instruct his followers as to how they should act in certain situations. The people were not educated so he told stories using parables. Parables are illustrations using daily life events to preach so that they would understand. Jesus' use of parables encouraged the people to have faith in God. We as Christians also have faith in God.

The Baptist faith starts by defining Salvation, which is freedom from the power and dominion of sin. It is predicated on the condition of repentance of wrong doing and faith in Jesus Christ. Roman 10:9-10 instructs us to confess with thy mouth Jesus as Lord and Savior and believe in thine heart that God raised him from the dead, and we will be saved. We then would have everlasting life (John 3:36). The natural body would die but the spirit would live on. Once saved the Holy Spirit comes to live in the believer to reveal truth of God. It is our counselor and comforter.

The Baptist church observes two Holy Ordinances, which are Baptism and Holy Communion. An ordinance is a ceremony that the Lord has presented and commanded the church to obey. These ordinances are observed once a month in the worship service. Baptism is a public showing of one's belief in Christ Jesus who died for our sins, was buried and rose on the third day. The believer is baptized by immersion in water to symbolize death to the life of sin. The candidate rises out of the water which symbolizes the resurrection in the new life in Christ. Jesus was baptized by John the Baptist and ask that we too be Baptized. The next ordinance is Holy Communion which is The Lord's Supper. It is the last meal Jesus shared with his disciples. He took bread and gave thanks and broke it and said that it is his body, which is for us and we are to do this in remembrance of him. He then took the cup of wine and said that it is the new covenant in his blood. We are to do this as a memorial to Jesus until he returns (1st Corinthians 11:23-26). Baptist celebrate the victory we have in Jesus and our eternal hope of everlasting life with Jesus. The elements of communion are broken bread and wine (grape juice). Communion is done once a month on the second Sunday at my church.

BAPTIST HISTORY:

The first Baptist was established in Amsterdam in the year of 1608 by John Smyth. The protestant reformation had just happened. John Smyth and Thomas Helwys believed that the church should consist of people who could testify about their own Christian conversion experience. They also believed that the state should not interfere with matters of the conscience. This belief led to religious liberty and the separation of church and state.[17] In America it was Roger Williams, a member of the Massachusetts Bay Colony who protested the government's control over religious affairs. He formed the colony of Rhode Island. Roger Williams formed the First Baptist Church in America in the year of 1639.[18]

BAPTIST POLITY

Baptist believe in religious freedom (Romans 13:1-7, Matthew 22:21, Acts 5:29, Matthew 10:28) Original Baptists did not tolerate a religious hierarchy or an episcopacy like that of bishops, overseers, cardinals, or the Pope. Each church is sovereign and autonomous. God is head of the church and the pastor is the under shepherd.[19]

---

[17] Brian Moynahan, *Faith: A HISTORY of Christianity* (New York, NY: Doubleday, 2002), 466.

[18] Brian Moynahan, *Faith: A History of Christianity* (NewYork, NY: Double day, 2002), 571.

[19] Ibid., 571.

The local Baptist church is free to handle and determine its own affairs.

According to David Kelsey (theologian) the New Testament is the history of Christianity. He suggests "that there are four ways to reflect theologically on the scripture; (1) as propositions about divine truth, (2) symbolic expressions of faith, (3) recitals of God's identity or (4) invitations to existential possibilities for new life".[20] Interpretation of the text is not standard. Baptist too, interpret the Bible according to their training and revelation from the supreme God. Every minister will have their own interpretation. It relates to materialism when pastors use the church for commercial reasons leading to personal gain other than that of a salary.

Is it permissible to use reason as a theological resource? According to some scholars, theologians have used reason to support certain truths. We are to take care in how we think about things. Can formal logic and mathematics be used in theology? According to the author reasoning is used in interpreting scripture, tradition and experience.[21] I would agree that some reasoning is acceptable, but is in opposition to Faith. When it comes to materialism we can probably find many reasons why we need to hold on to our tithes rather than give it to the church.

---

[20] Howard W. Stone and James O. Duke, *How To Think Theologically* (Mineapolis, MN: Fortress Press, 2002), 50.

[21] HowardW. Stoneand James O. Duke, *How To Think Theologically* (Mineapolis, MN: Fortress Press, 2013), 53.

The Sadducees or followers of Herod were liberal minded and false teachers. They took away from the word of God except the first five books of the Old Testament. They were free thinkers and rationalists who were secular and materialist-minded. They collaborated with the Romans to do away with Jewish culture but embraced Roman and Greek culture. They were rewarded with wealth and became known as the Sanhedrin (Matthew 16:1-12). Religionists in early days did not abandon materialism. They were warned as we are today to take heed of leaven at all times. God holds us responsible for all our actions because he has given us a guide through his word and the Holy Spirit that will lead and guide us into all truth. Materialism beyond what is necessary for us to exist is influenced by Satan and is against the will of God.

There are three dimensions of mankind. First we are a Spirit, born from above through the womb of a woman. We were born into sin through the fall of Adam (1Cor.5:7). Acceptance of Jesus as our Savior gave to us a new life in Christ. The second dimension is our soul which is our intellect, sensibilities, will and mind. It needs training through reading and studying the word of God (Romans 12) so that we are not conformed to the world but transformed by the renewing of our mind. The body (outward man) is the house we live in. We must not be ruled by our body but rather by the (inward man) Spirit. We now live and walk in the Spirit, and our life is directed by God to do his will. If we follow God's plans our needs will be met and we will not desire material goods beyond what we need to sustain us.

I support E.M. Bounds claim that the Church is a unique institution. It should seek to catch fish out of the sea not change the sea. The goal is to sanctify, purify and renew the sinner so that he or she can have eternal life. Trying to save the world sounds good but it makes the Church worldly. For what will it profit a man if he gains the whole world and loses his soul (Matthew 16:26)? The purpose of God's Church is Spiritual edification and not entertainment. The Church must not supply unsanctified desires.[22]

---

[22] E.M. Bounds, 54-59.

Psychological Perspective

Materialism in the church due to Spiritual warfare is in full force because people are not true to self. I will relate it to David Winnicott's theory of True Self False Self. He is a psychoanalyst. He did a study on the maturation process of infants. According to Winnicott, the False Self develops early in the infant-mother relationship but is not seen as a big problem in normal development. The child is dependent on the mother for survival so her behavior and attitude is essential. The stage of object-relationship starts with the mother. She is thought to be a good-enough mother by displaying unlimited power or authority, which is perceived by the infant. This gives strength to the infant's weak ego and gives rise to the true self after many repeats. If the mother is not good-enough, she does not meet the child's needs. The false self emerges due to the mother's inability to perceive the infant's needs. When the mother is good-enough the infant can start to believe in external reality that seems like magic to the child. The infant is able to relax and enjoy the illusion as he or she is able to perceive an object or symbol that is joined to mom. If the mother is not good enough the process of symbol usage is not started. The infant is isolated and lives falsely, because there are no external objects. The infant becomes irritable and bodily functions such as feeding are inhibited. The infant reacts to environmental demands. It builds false relationships that appear real so the infant becomes like the mother. The False Self functions by hiding the True Self by meeting environmental demands or by finding ways to enable the true-self.[23]

Elizabeth Johnson states that there is a revolution in theology because old concepts are stale and society needs transformation. The living God is limitless, so no matter how much we know, we can't conceive the mystery of God. The human heart is always searching. As God seekers, the spirit yearns deeper union with God. The ongoing quest is channeled by history and new circumstances. Rituals and constructs that pointed to God in one age don't make sense in the next.[24]

Gustavo Gutierrez, a Liberation theologian speaks about faith in an oppressed community. Faith demanded that no person should be dehumanized. Latin American Christians had suffered for thirty years at the hands of corrupt and brutal regimes. Liberation Theology encouraged some priests to align with guerrillas because two percent of the

---

[23] David Winnicott, *The Maturational Process and The Facilitating Environment* (New York, NY: Karnac Books ltd, 1990), 1.

[24] Elizabeth Johnson, *Quest for the Living God: Mapping Frontiers in the Theology of God* (New York, NY: Continuu m International Publishing Group ltd, 2007), 13.

population were in control of the resources. The Roman Church was expected to share the poverty of its flock. They stated that Catholic doctrine did not use property for public use. The "marginalized and oppressed", have surfaced to take steps to improve their life and acquire material wealth.[25] These people are in need of material goods to lift the people out of poverty.

Abraham Maslow's early life was one of frustration and sadness. His father was absent both physically and emotionally. He hated his mother and called her a schizophrenia who was ignorant and cruel. It was this experience that encouraged him to study psychological health and happiness. He devised a hierarchy of needs chart that must be fulfilled in order to be happy. The first tier is physiological needs such as breathing, food, drink, sleep, sex and excretion. The next tier safety which includes the body, employment, resources, morality, the family, health and property. The third tier is love and belonging needs, which includes friendship, family and sexual intimacy. The fourth tier is esteem needs that include self-esteem, confidence, achievement, respect of others and respect from others. The fifth tier is Self-Actualization. It includes acceptance of facts, lack of prejudice, problem solving, spontaneity, creativity and morality. Each tier should be fulfilled to insure happiness. Self-actualized people are satisfied with life. They are independent in their thinking. They are not hurtful or

---

[25] Brian Moynahan, *Faith: A History of Christianity* (New York, NY: Doubleday, 2002), 707.

sarcastic but have a sense of humor. They have a kinetic relationship with the human race.[26]

The second tier (lower) is safety. This tier could influence people to embrace materialism. A young person or couple rearing children might hold on to their money or resources to protect against an emergency like the loss of a job, family member, life savings or health insurance. Having more than enough gives them confidence.

---

[26] http://www.pursuit-of-happiness.org/history-of-happiness/abraham-maslow

Social and Cultural Analysis

I first attended my church in the early 1970s. The moral climate of the church was one of affluence and elegance. It felt like a high-society club. I did not consider it to be a problem because I worked for Columbia Broadcasting Services and made a lot of money. I would climb the ladder of success to become assistant supervisor of payroll processing. I was reared in a southern Baptist Church that promoted the idea of looking your best when you go to church. We did not have much money so we had few clothes, but what we had was kept clean. We had clothes that was worn only for church.

Bethany Baptist Church was the first black church to occupy the Stuyvesant area. The Pastor was very eloquent, tall, pleasing to the eye, educated and had an extraordinary voice. People followed him. A church adopts the ways and beliefs of the pastor because each church has freedom to govern as it decides. Doctor William Agustus Jones Jr., graduated with honors from the University of Kentucky and Crozier Theological Seminary in Chester Pennsylvania. He also studied at the University of Ghana at Legion. He earned a doctorate from Colgate Rochester Divinity School and later served as a visiting professor. Doctor Jones became pastor of Bethany on September 16, 1962. He was involved in civic organizations and fought for social justice in the neighborhood. I lived in the same neighborhood as he did and ran into him often. He led protests against the local A&P food market where we shopped because they did not employ black people. Jones appeared on radio and television and preached on every continent.

He became president of the Progressive National Baptist Convention (PNBC) and founded the National Black Pastor's Conference. He too served as National Chairman of SCLC's Operation Breadbasket. Pastor Jones led Bethany in the construction of the block-long stone Neo-Gothic church building that was completed in October 1967.[27] Pastor Jones stated often (in my hearing) that a free preacher in a free pulpit leading a free people is our motto. He did not accept money from politicians or the state. He did not want the church to be obligated to outsiders by accepting funds.

The standard was set high and Doctor Jones had accomplished much. Those who followed as leaders of Bethany had to be high achievers. The church consisted of lawyers, doctors, teachers, politicians and people from the upper middle class. There were people who frowned at

---

[27] Martha Simmons and Frank A. Thomas, eds., *PREACHING WITH SARCED FIRE: AN ANTHOLOGY OF AFRICAN AMERICAN SERMONS 1750 to THE PRESENT* (NewYork :WW. Norton&Company Inc., 2010), 746.

you if they thought that you were low class. I had been in Bethany for a very long time before the Spirit struck me and opened my eyes. I went from being a carnal Christian to a Spirit-filled Christian and taught new members class. I often heard people refer to Bethany as being a money church. The church was very traditional and did not welcome any change. For example, it was rare to shout or echo words of praise to God, I was fearful that I would be asked to be quiet.

I can say that Bethany was and still is a church that embraces materialism. The word of God is preached and some people are spirit filled but the majority of the members are carnal Christians, who don't understand things of the spirit.

Now God is seeking to perfect his church before Jesus return. Members are having a difficult time not being the center of attention and not doing what they have always done. People feel entitled to have the best and most in material goods and services. There is little consideration for the elderly and how they are to survive on Social security and pension fund monies. The new pastor is leading the church to become a New Testament church and it is good. He is putting the young people in leadership positions. Young people aspire to accomplish material wealth as a sign of their success. I too did the same when I was young with the idea that I wanted to have the American dream which includes a home and a nice car. These things are acceptable as long as it does not inflict hardship on the elderly and the church expenses are covered. 1 John 2:14-17 instructs us to love not the world, neither the things of the world. If we do the love of the Father is not in us.

The social and cultural history is very important in shaping the attitudes and accepted norms of the people. What worked for one generation will not be accepted by another. The word of God should never be compromised. In order for the young and old to be on the same page they will need to renew their minds by reading and studying the Bible (Romans 12). A renewed mind will also prevent a person from desiring things in excess.

Sister X

Date of visit: 02/19/2015

Length of visit: 30 minutes (6:00-6:30p.m.)

Preliminary Information:

The focus of my paper is Materialism in the Baptist Church due to spiritual warfare or greed. The person interviewed and I have a long history of visiting sick people in the hospital, at their home and in a rehabilitation facility. She is in a leadership position. I like and have great respect for this lady. I have never heard a negative remark coming from her. I called Sister X to ask if I could talk to her about our church and the transition process. She said that evil forces will enter our life and seek to deter us from our mission in life, but we must press on and be faithful to God.

Observations:

Sister X lives in Brooklyn with her family. She dresses corporate like. She is always professional and pleasant. I would link her to the title true Christian. I have known her more than thirty years and she has never mistreated or spoke ill of anyone in my presence.

Visit narrative   **C: Chaplain**   **P: Patient**

C1   Hello, Sister X, how are you feeling in this frigid weather?

P1   I am very well because I didn't go out into the cold. Do you want some hot tea?

C2   I'll just have some water, thank you.

P2   Good to see you, you know how much I love you and your husband.

C3   You are so kind. I want to talk to you about our church.

P3   OK. What's on your mind?

C4   You stated some time ago that the music is not reverent to you. Do you still hold the same opinion?

P4   It has toned down some. Words in a song are important because they minister to me. Reverence for God must be heard in a song because it is what feeds my spirit. The song "Pass me not O Gentle Savior", is a form of praying.

C5   Do you see the Church going in the right direction?

P5   Bible reading is falling away. We must stay steady in the Word to insure sound doctrine. We see signs of the end time. The parable of the fig tree spoken about in the Bible is before us, the weather is a good example. We must not let the Church go down. If we hold to God's unchanging hand his church will not fail. We can't let Satan have dominion over the church.

C6   Do you think that there is too much attention on money and material things?

P6   We must give as God has given to us. If the money is misused, it is not on us. God sees all things and will take care of those who misuse it. The way people dress is embedded in our history and slavery. As a people we had no outlet, so when we saved enough money to buy something pretty to wear to church it made us feel better about oneself. Church was the only place we could go so we wanted to look our best.

C7   How do you feel about the dress code?

P7   I leave it where it is and don't let it bother me. I don't put it on my plate.

C8   What about leadership in the Church?

P8   I am not affected. I pray all the time. I pray that people would say and do as they would if God is there.

C9   Do you think that there is too much of the world in the Church?

P9   A person must have respect for self to have respect for God. We need to represent God at all times. People might be turned away from the church by observing Christians who are doing wrong.

C10   What about disrespect for the elderly?

P10   I have not seen or experienced disrespect.

C11   Thanks so much for sharing your opinion regarding our Church.

P11   It was a pleasure and I hope that I have been helpful.[28]

---

[28] Sister X, interview by author, Brooklyn: NY, February 19, 2015.

Summary:

Sister X was very loving and spontaneous in her answer to my questions, she did not search for words. She was genuine and always chose the positive response. There was not one negative remark about the Church. Her theology is in line with her Baptist faith. I believe that life lived has afforded her the opportunity to see God in a transforming way. She understands that life will bring many hardships and devastating moments but God will be in the midst of it all. The holy other is visible to her in the midst of a crisis. She stated that she is concerned about others and their growth. A member of the Church for more than fifty years attest to the love and dedication she holds. Her endurance through tough times is attributed to continuous prayer and trust is God's faithfulness. She has left the natural state of mankind, which is lived without a Savior. The next step is the carnal life, which accepts the Savior but lives in one's own strength. The spirit being has accepted the Savior and is empowered by the Holy Spirit to live in harmony with God. This is her position as she is guided by this force. She said numerous times that it is important to not put things on your plate, but rather let things pass you by. She also said that when she taught school she bought quality clothes that would last a long time and she still wear those clothes. On occasions she sews an outfit but rarely goes into the stores. Sister X may have been a little naïve by not observing that idolatry is in the church. There is too much focus on money, status symbols and performance skills leading to competition. It is conceivable for young people to start thinking and planning for the golden years.

Sister X seem to foster a sense of self- empowerment gained from her strong faith. Her life is filled with caring for her family and the sick and shut-in. Her stability is nurtured by her obligation to family and the church. God is not this big force that does not relate to people but one that has compassion for people. She is able to communicate with all people as she intuitively sees where they are in their relationship with God. She has been retired for many years. Material loss does not affect her because she lives a simple life. Sister X taught Sunday school and is in a leadership position in the church, therefore there is no role loss as a retired teacher. There might be a systemic loss due to changes in the function of the church. Sister X might be in denial of all the changes and this is how she deals with her anxiety. I would say that she is her true self in accordance with Winnicott's theory of true self/false self. An infant matures into the true self if the mother is good-enough and nourishes the infant's weak ego and the child is able to believe in external objects.

Sister X does not see her role as a female, senior citizen and an African American to be a disadvantage. She is well educated and taught middle age students. Her abilities are utilized in her church. Her accomplishments within society and her culture has given her power to continue as a leader. Faith is the glue that has kept her focused. Sister X's family dynamics has given her stability.

Self-evaluation:

Sister X is the only person in the Church with this attitude I thought. Perhaps this is the best example of one who walks in the spirit because the mind has been renewed according to Romans 12. It is Holy living and the ability to discern the will of God. Through the reading and studying of the Word of God one learns to let go of material things in excess. This lady became my measuring rod. I have been called as a Minister to help people, but I have a lot more to learn. Initially I thought that I should try harder, but know that prayer is sufficient. I do need to listen intently to that inner voice of correction. I am a prayer intercessor on behalf of my family, the homeless and all who enter my space but I still have a lot of dross that must be removed. I also have to work on having too many material goods. The ultimate goal is to reflect the nature of Jesus.

Sister X exemplified the Grace of God. People in leadership positions in the church say and do unrighteous things repeatedly. This suggest to me that they don't care and are aware of their behavior. It is about politics and positions.

I spoke to a younger person in Bethany who believed that there is materialism in the church but will leave it to God to correct. She is very simple in her church attire and is very thrifty. She earns a three figure salary but is not obsessed with material things. All she needs is the basic necessities to survive. Her focus is on having a peaceful and low stress life.

I believe that there is materialism in Bethany Baptist Church due to evil influence.

I am also guilty of this practice and will seek to bring it in control. There are so many organizations that need help, especially the homeless.

Future plans:

I plan on sharing more and getting more involved with people who are in need of material goods. Maybe this topic of research is for my enlightenment. I will share this subject matter with all those who will listen. I hope to be able to influence the Church to share the wealth with those in need in the community and the Kingdom of God.

Bibliography

Borg, Marcus J. and John Dominic Crossan. *The First Paul: Reclaiming the RadicalVisionary Behind theChurch's Conservative Icon*. NewYork: HarperOne, 2009.

Bounds, E. M. *Guide To Spiritual Warfare*. PA: Whitaker House, 1984.

Closson, Don. *The Stairway to Heaven: Materialism and the Church*. http://www.leaderu.com/orgs/probe/docs/stairway.html.

Doehring, Carrie. *The Practice of Pastoral Care: a post modern approach*. Kentucky: John Knox Press, 2006.

Hendricks, Obery M. *The Politics of Jesus*. New York: Three Leaves Press, 2006.

Internal Journal of Business and Social Science.Vol.2 no.23 (special issue (December 2011: 241.

Johnson, Elizabeth. *Quest for the Living God: Mapping Frontiers in the Theology of God*. New York: Continuum International Publishing Group ltd, 2007.

Joines, Vannand I an Stewart.*Personality Adaptations:A new Guide to Human Understanding in Psychology and Counselling*. North Carolina: Life Space Publishing, 2002.

Moynahan, Brian. *Faith: A History of Christianity*. NewYork: Double day, 2002.

Shelley Bruce. *The Millionaire and the Dreamer*. http://www.leaderu.com/orgs/probe/docs/stairway.html.

Simmons,Martha.and FrankA.Thomas. *PREACHING WITH SACRED FIRE: AN ANTHOLOGY OF AFRICAN AMERICAN SERMONS, 1750 TO THE PRESENT:* New York: W.W. Norton & Company, 2010.

Stone, Howard W. and James O. Duke. *How to Think Theologically 3rd. ed.* Minneapolis: Fortress Press, 1996.

Willis, Cecil. *"Problems in The Church (iii): Materialism" truth Magazine,* November, 1962. http://www.truthmagazine.com/archives/volume7/TM007013.htm.

Winnicott, David. *The Maturational Processes and The Facilitating Environment:* NewYork: Karnac Books ltd, 1990.

Printed in the United States
By Bookmasters